Rijksmuseum
Stadhouderskade 42; Tel: 02

Amsterdam became one of the world's great cities during the first three-quarters of the 17th century — a 75-year era Dutch historians fondly refer to as the "Golden Age." It was during this period that the Netherlands established colonies worldwide and created a vast and extremely lucrative network of trade routes. Leading the expansion efforts were the Dutch West India Company, which controlled Holland's trade with colonists in the Americas, and the Dutch East India Company, which controlled the country's trade with colonists in Indonesia, Africa and Asia. Both of these companies had their headquarters in Amsterdam, the port city to which most of the trade ships returned. The wealth that poured into Amsterdam during the Golden Age radically transformed the city. It was then that most of Amsterdam's canals and grandiose buildings were constructed (see annotation 23). It was then that the city's streets were paved with cobblestones and the canals were lined with elegant homes belonging to the newly affluent merchant class. And it was then that Amsterdam's nouveaux riches commissioned artists to paint their portraits. The Dutch Masters, as these artists would later be known, included Frans Hals, Pieter Saenredam, Jacob van Ruisdael, Willem Claesz Heda, Jan Steen and, most importantly, Jan Vermeer and Rembrandt van Rijn.

Masterpieces by all of these artists are on display at the Rijksmuseum, which ranks with the Louvre, the Hermitage and the Uffizi as one of the major museums of European painting, sculpture and decorative arts. The Rijksmuseum's collection presents a superb picture of the richly varied painting of the Golden Age, from still-lifes by Heda to Dutch river landscapes by Ruisdael to domestic scenes by Pieter de Hooch. But the biggest crowd pleasers by far are the works by Vermeer and Rembrandt. Vermeer is represented with four paintings, including one of the Rijksmuseum's best-known paintings, The Kitchen Maid, which depicts a maid pouring milk into a bowl. It is considered a great artwork for the way Vermeer used light to suggest reality. The astute viewer will notice that the wicker basket on the wall behind the maid reflects light dully, in contrast to the gleaming copper dish beside it; these are clearly very different materials, as evidenced by the ways the sunlight from a nearby window plays upon them. The astute viewer will also notice the attention to detail Vermeer gave the bread on the table, the nail in the wall, the broken windowpane. You would not be the first person to remark that his detail work could pass for photography. The museum has 19 paintings by Rembrandt, including major works such as The Night Watch (famous for its feeling of movement and for its many illusions; the captain's hand, for example, seems to be extending forward out of the painting); The Jewish Bride (remarkable in that it shows Rembrandt used paint to create not only color but also relief; he used a brush and a small amount of paint for the faces and hands, for example, and he used globs of paint applied with a palette knife for the clothes, giving the clothes actual texture); and, The Syndics of the Drapers' Guild (noteworthy for Rembrandt's grouping of six stern subjects in such a way as to avoid creating a stilted portrait and to remove the appearance of five hats in a row). Also at the Rijksmuseum are four other departments: sculpture and decorative arts, Dutch history, the national print room, and Asiatic art. The Rijksmuseum is a must-see attraction!

Details: Daily, 10–5. Cost: fff/ee. Signage is in Dutch and English.

 Van Gogh Museum
Paulus Potterstraat 7; Tel: 020/570-5200 (www.vangoghmuseum.nl)

During the late 19th century a handful of talented artists deviated from the naturalistic accuracy of Impressionism and embraced a freely expressive use of color and form. Or put another way, they chucked the practice of copying nature in favor of mental conception in art. These artists have been aptly categorized by art historians as post-Impressionists, and it was from them that the modern-art movements of Surrealism, Futurism, Cubism, Expressionism and

Fauvism were born. The impact these artists — Vincent van Gogh, Paul Cézanne, Camille Pissaro, Paul Gauguin, Georges Seurat and Henri de Toulouse-Lautrec — had on subsequent European and American artists cannot be overstated. They are nothing less than the founders of modern art. Which of these men had the most influence or talent is, like post-Impressionism itself, a matter of subjectivity. But in the Netherlands, at least, the opinion is unanimous: the greatest artist of the 19th century was van Gogh (van Gogh, coincidentally, was the only Dutchman of the group; all of the other artists were French). Incredibly, van Gogh never tried his hand at painting until he was in his late twenties. Before then he'd been a salesman, a French tutor, a theological student and an evangelist — positions that brought him little satisfaction. At wit's end, he would later write, he developed an urge to leave mankind "some memento in the form of drawings or paintings — not made to please any particular movement, but to express a sincere human feeling." When van Gogh decided to become an artist, no one, not even he himself, suspected that he had extraordinary gifts. In the decade that followed, van Gogh produced 1,100 drawings and almost 900 paintings.

What makes the collection at the spacious Van Gogh Museum so exceptional — in addition to being the largest van Gogh collection in the world — is that it contains representative works illustrating each period in the artist's career. During his earliest period — his "Dutch period" (1869–1885) — his drawings and paintings depicted human labor and related themes (and it was in Nuenen, Holland, that he painted his first great picture, The Potato Eaters). His vibrant use of colors came later, when he left Holland in 1885 for Antwerp, then France to seek a more stimulating atmosphere. Between bouts of madness and depression that more than once drove him to enter an asylum, van Gogh produced mostly gorgeous and uplifting landscapes and paintings of flowers. Then, on July 27, 1890, just after completing his ominous Wheatfield With Crows, van Gogh shot himself in the chest in Auvers-sur-Oise, France. The artist's remarkable and tragic life ended two days later. He was 37. Ironically, it was not until long after his death that he received the recognition he so richly deserved. In fact, he sold only a single painting while alive. Today, the Van Gogh Museum contains more than 200 paintings, 580 drawings, seven sketchbooks and 750 letters the artist wrote to his brother. The collection also includes works by van Gogh's contemporaries, particularly those artists who directly influenced van Gogh's work. The Van Gogh Museum is a stellar attraction, made even more so by a mega-million dollar renovation that added a dramatic **new wing**, clad in stone and titanium steel, for special exhibits.

While at the Van Gogh Museum, take note of the **Women of Ravensbruck Monument** in the plaza, dedicated to the 100,000 women who died at Ravensbruck concentration camp — the only concentration camp the Nazis built that housed only women. The moving memorial is inscribed: "For her who until the bitter end refused to accept fascism."

Details: Daily, 10–5. Cost: fff/ee. Signage is in Dutch and English.

3 Stedelijk Museum of Modern Art
Paulus Potterstraat 13; Tel: 020/573-2737 (www.stedelijk.nl)

Within a brief walk of the Rijksmuseum and the Van Gogh Museum is this contemporary art museum of world renown. The Stedelijk organizes exhibitions and collections in the field of modern art, from the latter part of the 19th century to the present. The museum's collection is a many-sided one: it includes not only paintings and sculpture, prints and drawings, but also photographs, videos, applied art, industrial designs and posters. Some "classics" of modern art — van Gogh, Cézanne, Picasso, Monet, Manet, Matisse and Chagall — are often shown in the Stedelijk. Works by Piet Mondrian and Kasimir Malevich, important founders of abstract art, are always on view here. In fact, some 50 paintings, gouaches and drawings by Malevich, representing the largest collection of Malevichs outside of Russia, constitute one of the highlights of the collection. In particular, his foray into Suprematism, a highly geometric style of abstract painting, can be studied better at the Stedelijk than anywhere else. Works by the famous modern Dutch painters Karel Appel and Willem de Kooning and the American artist Andy Warhol can also be viewed at the Stedelijk most of the time. There are works by several dozen other significant modern artists on display, as well as lots of pop art that begs the question, "Is this really art?" You be the judge. Regardless of the artistic value of some of the works on exhibit, the Stedelijk is always a fun and yet puzzling visit. Where else can you find under the same roof such a wonderfully pleasing painting like Matisse's The Parakeet and the Mermaid and the highly suspect work Plywood Piece by Donald Judd?

Details: Apr.-Oct., daily, 11–5; Nov.-Mar., daily, 10–6. Cost: fff/ee. Signage is in Dutch and English.

4 ## Concertgebouw
Concertgebouwplein 2–6; Tel: 020/675-4411(hotline); 020/671-8345 (box office)

The Netherlands' premier concert hall, designed by AL van Gendt in 1888, is the place to see the world's best conductors, the best soloists and the best orchestras – including its own Royal Concertgebouw Orchestra – in a near acoustically perfect setting (the Grote Zaal or Great Hall; the smaller Kleine Zaal is used for recitals). The honor of appearing on the Grote Zaal stage has been shared by the most famous names in the classical music biz. Take in a performance for a truly magical experience.

Details: Box office: Daily, 10–6:15. You can get the schedule of performances and purchase tickets on the Concertgebouw website (www.concertgebouw.com).

5 ## Vondelpark
(enter off Stadhouderskade, three blocks west of Rijksmuseum)

This 120-acre park, landscaped in English style, is filled with ponds, winding paths and sculpture. It's a great place to escape the hustle and bustle of the city and have a picnic, take a stroll, hop on that most Dutch of contraptions – the bicycle – or perhaps don some rollerblades. Park highlights include the outdoor theater (for free open-air concerts in July and Aug.) and the Teahouse (for coffee). One of the 19th-century entertainment pavilions, set on the northeastern edge of the park, is now home to the **Nederlands Filmmuseum** (Netherlands Film Museum), which screens classics from its extensive archives, plus has a great cafe (Vondelpark 3; call for screening schedule; tel: 020/589-1400).

Details: Take advantage of the park during the day only.

6 ## P.C. Hooftstraat

This posh shopping street is Amsterdam's version of New York's Fifth Avenue, London's Old Bond St., or Paris's Avenue George V. You can pick up the finest of ties, shoes, dresses and more at the top designer stores that line this upscale buyer's heaven. Even if you don't want to part with any cash, it's still a fun stroll. If you want to purchase a sparkler or two, head to nearby Coster Diamonds, one of Amsterdam's oldest diamond factories and the spot where the famous Koh-i-Noor diamond, part of the British Crown Jewels, was cut (diamonds for sale; prices are competitive but not great; Paulus Potterstraat 2; tel: 020/676-2222). Diamonds have been big biz in this city since the Sephardic Jews introduced the art of cutting when they arrived in the 16th century.

Details: Store hours are generally Mon. afternoons, Tues. to Fri., 9–6, Sat., 9–5.

7

Heineken Reception Center
Stadhouderskade 78; Tel: 020/523-9666

It's a pity all reception centers aren't like this one. "The Haystack," as Heineken employees fondly call it, dates to 1592. The enormous brick facility originally opened as a brewery and had been supplying Amsterdammers with beer for 272 years before Gerard Adriaan Heineken bought the facility in 1864 and began producing beers bearing his family name. In its headiest days — those just prior to its closing in 1988 — the brewery was producing more than a million hectoliters annually. Economic considerations spurred Heineken's directors to move production to breweries in Den Bosch and Zoeterwoude, but the company chose not to sell the historic building and instead decided to see what kind of tourist interest it would generate. In 1991, three years after the brewery was shut down, the site reopened as the Heineken Reception Center. It was a wise decision. Today, the reception center is one of the top tourist attractions in Amsterdam, even though, as a brewery, it's an empty barrel, so to speak. Scores of visitors wander through the Haystack daily, delivered in oversize touring buses that line up in front of the center's entrance. The visitors are treated to an explanation of the brewing process and are shown a film that takes the viewer through 5,000 years of brewing history in under five minutes. Then it's on to see the old, tiled brewery with its huge brewing coppers, and on to the stables where Heineken keeps dray horses just as it did a century ago. Last but not least, visitors are offered two much-appreciated beers, proving once again that two heads are better than one.

Details: Tours: Mon. to Fri., 9:30 and 11 (extra tours given at 1 and 2:30 between June 1 and Sept. 15). Visitors must be 18 or older. Cost: fff/ee (all proceeds go to charity). Arrive at least 20 minutes early.

Leidseplein
At the intersection of Leidsestraat and Lijnbaansgracht

The Leidseplein is an enormously popular square that's at the heart of Amsterdam's premier entertainment area. Historically, the square was a parking lot on the edge of town. Farmers used to park their carts where the bustling square is now situated before entering the city through a massive gate that has long since been demolished. Today, fire-eaters, musicians and jugglers fill the square during the day, performing for pocket change before usually large crowds. At night the square is jammed with young Amsterdammers who descend on the many bars, cafés and theaters in and around the square. An excellent and elegant place to enjoy a drink or grab a bite, even in casual (but certainly not grungy) clothes, is the **Café Americain** *inside the massive, can't-miss Americain Hotel at Leidsekade 97. The café is decorated in Art Deco, from the breathtaking suspended lights and the stained-glass windows to the tables and chairs used by patrons. Its wow factor on a scale of 1–10 among Art Deco admirers is a solid 10. An impressive buffet is available. Another famous cultural fixture in the area of Leidseplein is* **De Melkweg (Milky Way)**, *which is a multimedia center situated in a former dairy. Here you'll find movie theaters, a photographic gallery, even a very popular dance club with live music most nights (Lijnbaansgracht 234; tel: 020/624-1777). Also in the neighborhood is the* **Holland Casino** *(with everything from slots to roulette; Max Euweplein 62; tel: 020/620-1006) and the ever-popular* **Hard Rock Cafe** *(Max Euweplein 57; tel: 020/523-7625). Leidseplein is a good distance from the center of town, but well worth making an effort to reach.*

Details: The Leidseplein is served by many trolleys.

Museum van Loon
Keizersgracht 672 (near Vijzelstraat); Tel: 020/624-5255

This former home of the locally famous van Loon family gives the visitor a wonderful glimpse of high-society life in Amsterdam from the 17th century to the mid-20th century. The house itself dates from 1672, when it was designed and built by Adriaan Dortsman for the Flemish merchant Jeremias van Raey. In the years that followed, the magnificent patrician house — one of a matching pair — had numerous owners before it was acquired in 1884 by Willem van Loon, who became mayor of Amsterdam two years later. The house was owned by members of the van Loon family until 1945. After years of neglect and following 11 years of extensive renovations, the house opened as a museum in 1974. Visitors are treated to period rooms filled with ornately decorated furnishings, paneling, fireplaces, chandeliers, rugs and porcelain. On the walls are more than 80 van Loon family portraits, and among the treasures on display are a family album and commemorative coins that were struck in honor of seven golden wedding anniversaries celebrated by van Loon family members between 1621 and 1722. Outside, there's a formal rose garden and a stately 18th-century coach house.

Details: Fri. to Mon., 11–5. Cost: ff/e.

Tropenmuseum (Museum of the Tropics)
Linnaeusstraat 2 (at Mauritskade); Tel: 020/568-8215 (www.kit.nl/tropenmuseum)

The Tropenmuseum is the largest anthropological museum in the Netherlands, and it's a real beauty. The expansive, four-level museum is maintained by the Royal Tropical Institute, a foundation devoted to the study of cultures found only in the Tropics and Subtropics. Unlike your usual anthropological museum, where most of the displays consist of photographs and artifacts placed behind glass, here thousands of objects are creatively exhibited in walk-through city-street scenes and model villages. In the India section, for example, shops that look like they were plucked from a street in Calcutta line a corridor. As you meander past them, it takes little imagination to feel like you're in India. Fully costumed mannequins add to the realism. Likewise, in the African section, roadside markets have been re-created. Beside the many artifacts and handicrafts are well-thought-out signs in Dutch and English explaining the histories and uses of the objects you're looking at. In the Central Asia section, a yurta (a house used by nomadic shepherds) has been constructed that visitors are welcome to exam-ine. Signs describe in vivid detail how the homes are assembled and how they serve their owners' needs. Did you know that an imaginary line runs through the yurta, dividing the tent house into a women's half and a men's half? You would if you visited the Tropenmuseum. A visitor can easily spend a couple of days in this museum, learning lots about the many peoples who live in Indonesia, Southeast Asia, tropical Africa, tropical Latin America and elsewhere. This is a first-rate museum. Also on the premises is a giftshop selling a unique collection of artifacts and utensils, a restaurant where you can sample authentic tropical dishes, and a library housing many books on the Tropics and Subtropics.

Details: Mon. to Fri., 10–5, Sat., Sun., 12–5. Cost: fff/ee. Signage in Dutch and English.

Artis (Amsterdam Zoo)
Plantage Kerklaan 38-40; Tel: 020/523-3400 (www.artis.nl)

Founded in 1838, the Artis is the oldest zoo in the Netherlands. It is a place of great tranquility, with lots of lush gardens, meandering waterways and trees filled with tropical birds — a won-derful escape from the bustling, bicyclist-packed streets of Amsterdam and highly recom-mended if you feel you could really use a break from the action. But if you've ever been to one of the world's truly great zoos, where all of the animals live in spacious enclosures and eat better than most people, the Artis won't knock your socks off. Yes, it can boast that it has more than 900 species and offers an overview of the entire animal kingdom. And, yes, it's got a planetarium and a geological museum that are really impressive. But many of the enclosures need replacing and seeing big cats in small compounds, for example, isn't the kind of thing any animal lover wants to see. Fortunately, the zoo has plans to expand with the aim of offering the animals more living space. Inadequate space for some animals isn't a concern of most children, and this zoo is a terrific place to take kids. There is a children's farm and an incubator house. The Penguin Rock is also a major child pleaser, but then who doesn't like watching these adorable creatures. Another big hit is the beaver compound, which opened in 1992 and is thoroughly appreciated by its busy Canadian occupants. Also very entertaining are the inhabitants of Artis's three ponds — flamingoes, ducks, cranes, cormorants, swans, geese and other birds — that are free to fly about the zoo and frequently do. The zoo's restaurant overlooks a pond filled with Chilean flamingoes and is a super place to have lunch.

Details: Daily 9–5. Cost: fff/ee.

Hollandse Schouwburg
Plantage Middenlaan 24 (at Plantage Kerklaan); Tel: 020/626-9945

The story of Hollandse Schouwburg is one of sorrow and horror. Once a beautiful 19th-century theater and the cultural center of Amsterdam's thriving Jewish community, Hollandse Schouwburg will forever be remembered for its more recent history. The Nazis invaded the Netherlands in 1940, and in June 1942 they told Amsterdam's Jewish leaders that the city's Jews would take part in the German war-economy program. The Nazis duped the Jewish leaders into believing the city's Jewish population would be shipped to Germany to work in factories and would be allowed to return to their homes after the war. In fact, the German plan called for total extermination, but of course the Jewish leaders did not know this. Under such euphemisms as "emigration" and "compulsory work in Germany," the Nazis mislead Dutch Jews. The Jewish leaders unwittingly helped carry out these measures by instructing Amsterdam's Jews to report to the theater they knew so well. There, they were placed in trucks and taken to trains, which in turn took them first to Westerbork transit camp, then to the death camps of Auschwitz, Sobibor, Theresienstadt and Bergen-Belsen. In all, approximately 104,000 Dutch Jews were murdered this way (the Dutch Jewish population was estimated to be around 140,000). Only 6,000 of Amsterdam's Jews who reached the death camps got out alive. After the war the one-time theater was left to rot. Then, in 1962, a garden was planted in the former auditorium. Later a basalt column with a base in the shape of a Star of David was erected where the stage had been. Behind the column, chiseled into a block wall, are the words: "To the memory of those taken from here." In 1993 the theater's façade and foyer were restored. On the ground floor an eternal flame illuminates a memorial bearing the family names of the victims. Upstairs are scores of photos of Holland's Jewish community during the early 1940s. There are lots of group shots, and sadly, everyone was smiling for the camera.

Details: Daily, 11–4. Cost: Free.

Hortus Botanicus (Botanical Garden)
Plantage Middenlaan 2a; Tel: 020/625-9021

Amsterdam's Hortus Botanicus is one of the oldest botanical gardens in the world. This living museum dates from 1638 and was constructed at its present location around 1682. The garden contains some 250,000 flowers and 115,000 plants and trees from about 8,000 varieties. Many of the plants are threatened with extinction in their countries of origin. Much of the outdoor garden is occupied by plants whose natural habitat is temperate or Arctic. And found outdoors are a rock garden, a pond, numerous trees that were planted during the 1890s, an abundance of shrubs and an herb garden. Also on the grounds is a 19th-century palm house that contains a collection of rare cycad palms, a few of which are believed to be more than 300 years old. Elsewhere on the premises are a Mexican/Californian Desert House, a Butterflies House, and a Three-Climates Glasshouse that contains plants from the Subtropics, the Tropics and from African deserts. There is a gift shop near the entrance as well as an orangery where visitors are encouraged to stop for a cup of coffee or tea.

Details: Mon. to Fri., 9–5, Sat. and Sun., 11–5 (to 4 from Oct.–Mar.). Cost: ff/e.

 ### Joods Historisch Museum (Jewish Historical Museum)
Jonas Daniël Meijerplein 2 (facing Waterlooplein); Tel: 020/626-9945 (www.jhm.nl)

*Chronicling the Jewish experience in the Netherlands, this museum is striking for both its setting and contents. Perched on the edge of what was **once Amsterdam's Jewish Quarter**, the Jewish Historical Museum is housed in four contiguous 17th and 18th-century synagogues, all restored to perfection after near total destruction by the Nazis. The museum's collection traces the history of Jews in Holland from the arrival of the first Jews in Amsterdam to the present. Thoughtful displays of art and artifacts such as antique Torahs, and signage in English and Dutch, tell the history of Holland's Jews in an eloquent and captivating manner. Most intriguing to visitors are the displays relating the details of life for Jews in the Netherlands under Nazi occupation. Here, we see many of the same kind of photos on display at the Hollandse Schouwburg: nurses taking a break from their duties, children attending class, men at streetside enjoying a cigarette, a young couple being married. Little remains of the buildings in the Jewish Quarter, most having been destroyed during the war (some buildings were razed to build the Muziektheater). This museum is well worth a special trip!*

Details: Daily, 11–5. Cost: ff/e.

 ### Portuguese Synagogue
Mr. Visserplein 3 (opposite Joods Historisch Museum); Tel: 020/624-5351

Standing in the old Jewish Quarter, opposite the Jewish Historical Museum, is this grand 17th-century synagogue … Amsterdam's most important Jewish relic and one of the most famous synagogues in the world. Rumor has it that the synagogue survived the Nazi occupation at the behest of Spain's General Franco who, out of respect to his mother (who allegedly was Jewish), asked Hitler to spare it. Saved from destruction, this synagogue was restored in the 1950s and looks as it did 300+ years ago. Its roots date to 1492, when Spain expelled its Jewish citizens (many fled to Portugal but were nevertheless forcibly baptized after 1496). More than a century later, descendants of these Spanish victims of the Inquisition who wanted to live as Jews began to arrive in Amsterdam, where they established a neighborhood east of center. At that time the Netherlands was at war with Spain, so as to avoid being identified with the Spanish enemy these refugees called themselves Portuguese Jews. In 1671 the Portuguese Jewish community began work on this exquisite, Ionic-style synagogue, which was inaugurated on Aug. 2, 1675 (the date of 1672 inscribed in gilt Hebrew lettering above the entrance was chiseled prematurely and has yet to be corrected). With the completion of the synagogue, the Portuguese Jews could finally worship as they wished after nearly 200 years of persecution. Among the noteworthy attractions: the brass chandeliers that are unique to the Netherlands for their size (with more than 1,000 candles, these provide the only lighting for the synagogue); the eternal flame, which commemorates the seven-branched candelabrum that burned continually in the Temple in Jerusalem; and the 12 stone columns supporting the women's galleries (separate seating areas for women during services), which represent the Twelve Tribes of Israel.

Details: Apr.–Oct., Sun. to Fri., 10–12:30 and 1–4; Nov.–Mar., Mon. to Thurs., 10–12:30 and 1–4, Fri., 10–3, Sun., 10–12. Cost: ff/e.

16 ## Waterlooplein Flea Market
Waterlooplein (behind the enormous Muziektheater & Stadhuis)

There once was a time when Amsterdam's foremost outdoor market was a place where beautiful antiques and museum-quality artworks could frequently be found. Those days have gone the way of the large flightless bird of Mauritius, the dodo. Today, the quality of goods to be found at Waterlooplein runs from bad to worse to simply ridiculous. Complementing the cheap clothing, the boxes of old records, a kid selling camouflage wear, and so forth is a fast-food wagon that sells French fries covered with mayonnaise — perfect food for the situation. So why even mention this place at all? Well, as they say, one person's garbage is another person's treasure. If you've been looking for a purple leather jacket with the Pink Panther's mug stitched across the back, this is the kind of place that might have it. In fact, you never know what kind of junk — er, treasures — you might come across here. So, if you can afford the time and if you've got the inclination, come on down.

*Adjacent to the flea market is the **Holland Experience**. Twenty years ago this thing would have been really something. Or, put another way, if you're from a country that's technologically 20 years behind the times, you'll be in for a treat. Holland Experience is a motion-simulation experience that takes place in a small cinema, only at this cinema all of the seats are situated on a hydraulically controlled platform. As a short film promoting Holland gets rolling, the screen lights up with images of a jetliner taking off. At the same time, the hydraulics jiggle the seats, weakly simulating the feeling of take off. During another point in the film, which introduces the viewer to pleasing Dutch landscapes and attractions, the camera hones in on some sausages and within seconds the cinema fills with the smell of — yes — sausages. You get the idea. The experience is more cute than impressive, but you'll see ads for it throughout Amsterdam (Waterlooplein 17; daily, 10–10; Cost: fff/ee; tel: 020/422-2233).*

Details: Daily, 9–5.

 ## Museum het Rembrandthuis (Rembrandt's House)
Jodenbreestraat 4; Tel: 020/520-0400 (www.rembrandthuis.nl)

The Museum het Rembrandthuis is situated in the house Rembrandt van Rijn shared with his wife, Saskia, their son, Titus, and his mistress, Hendrickje, from 1639 to 1658. It is also where the artist had his studio, and it is believed that he painted The Night Watch *under a lean-to in the courtyard beside the old house in 1642. He spent lavishly to decorate his home and, though his work was constantly sought, he could never "paint" his way out from under his bills, and he died in abject poverty on Oct. 4, 1669. Rembrandt's masterpieces, including* The Night Watch, *are located at the Rijksmuseum, but the Museum het Rembrandthuis, which was restored to its original condition in early 1999, remains the only place in the world with a permanent exhibition of Rembrandt's etchings. In fact, the Museum het Rembrandthuis has 250 of the 290 prints credited to the artist. Among his most highly regarded works on display here are* Interior With Saskia Laying in Bed, Adam and Eve, *and* Beggars Receiving Alms at the Door of a House. *In addition to the artworks, visitors also have the opportunity to see a short film about Rembrandt's life and his art. Also on display are temporary exhibitions, most of which are closely related to Rembrandt's professional life. There is a giftshop and a café on the premises as well. Even if you see the Rijksmuseum, it is well worth your while to visit the Museum het Rembrandthuis. It is here, and only here, that you can really get a feel for Rembrandt the husband, Rembrandt the teacher, Rembrandt the collector of art and curiosities. The artist, of course, won't be there, but as you walk through the wonderfully maintained home where he spent most of his adult life you'll feel that he's only slipped out for a moment.*

Details: Mon. to Sat., 10–5, Sun., 1–5. Cost: fff/ee.

Muziektheater (Opera House)
Waterlooplein 22 (next to the Amstel River); Tel: 020/625-5455

*The Netherlands has two world-class performance companies (the National Ballet and the Netherlands Opera), both of of which perform at the 1,689-seat Muziektheater, which opened in 1986 following enormous controversy. The Muziektheater was built at the same time as the adjacent **Stadhuis** (City Hall). To make room for them at their present site, dozens of medieval houses representing the majority of the surviving homes of the original Jewish Quarter had to be destroyed. The destruction of the historic homes triggered violent clashes between protesters and police, and more than a few tourists were inadvertently sickened by tear gas. The final outcome was an extremely popular and fairly spectacular-looking opera house and a rather unpopular and altogether unattractive city hall. The Muziektheater's appearance is defined by its glass-and-marble exterior, its sweeping red-carpeted staircases, and its mostly soft-pink color scheme. The sound and lighting equipment is state-of-the-art, but surprisingly the auditorium's acoustics are second-rate and experts' efforts to improve them did little to help. There are architectural blunders backstage as well: the ceilings in the ballet rehearsal rooms are so low that dancers can't practice lifts, someone forgot to give the orchestra a room in which to rehearse, and the scenery lifts were placed away from the loading entrances (a problem that has since been rectified). Still, it's the performances that visitors come for, and there's nothing disappointing about them.*

Details: Contact the Muziektheater box office for a schedule of upcoming performances. The opera house may be reached by e-mail (info@het-muziektheater.nl). Tickets can be purchased one month in advance. Cost: fff/eee.

 Jewish Resistance Fighters Memorial
Near the Stadhuis, where the Amstel River meets the Zwanenburgwal

*An estimated 16,000 Jews managed to hide from the Nazis in and around Amsterdam. To those who helped the Jews escape their mortal enemy, and to the Jews who resisted the Nazis at great peril, a black marble statue has been erected in their honor at the edge of the former Jewish Quarter. Understandably, there was little the Dutch Jews and people sympathetic to their plight could do to resist the Nazis. The Nazis had the weapons and the hatred to use them, and the Jews did not know where the deportation trains they were ordered into headed. People who resisted Nazi orders were usually executed and their deaths announced as warnings to others. And as victim Juliette Binger noted in her memoirs, "Go into hiding? I would only be a danger to those who wanted to help me." Still, efforts were made: Some resisters published an underground newspaper, some engaged in sabotage, some reported Nazi activities to the Allies via illegal radio contact. Most of these actions were conducted by non-Jews who weren't as closely watched as the Jews. The sympathizers were most helpful to Amsterdam's Jewish population by hiding them in their homes and workplaces at enormous personal risk. Among these courageous people were Victor Kugler, Johannes Kleiman, Miep Gies and Bep Voskuijl, non-Jews who assisted Anne Frank's family and other Jews for nearly two years. There were many other non-Jews who did what they could to help Jews escape deportation. Without their help, every one of Amsterdam's Jews would have been sent to concentration camps. The story of the Dutch resistance is told in detail at the **Verzetsmuseum** (near Hollandse Schouwburg, see annotation 12; Plantage Kerklaan 61; Tues. to Fri., 10–5, Sat. and Sun., 12–5; Cost: fff/ee; Tel: 020/620-2535).*

Details: The German effort to rout hiding Jews was led by the dreaded Gestapo, which had its local headquarters in an imposing brick building one mile south of the Rijksmuseum. The building still stands, occupied by the Gerritt van der Veen School. A small memorial is the only hint of the evil that had once existed there.

Museum Willet-Holthuysen
Herengracht 605 (near Amstel); Tel: 020/523-1870

Like the Museum van Loon, the Museum Willet-Holthuysen offers the visitor a good look into life among Amsterdam's upper crust from the 17th to 19th centuries. This particular house was built in 1687, but the museum takes its name from Abraham Willet and his wife Louisa Holthuysen, who lived in this elegant double canal house during the late 19th century. Louisa outlived her husband and upon her death in 1895 she left her house, its contents and her applied-art collection to the city. Her legacy was accepted and a year later the museum officially opened. Today, visitors are treated to simply spectacular rooms filled with elegant wall hangings, Dresden china, paintings by Jacob de Wit, many gilded mirrors and lots of French furniture. The garden is designed like an early 18th-century French symmetrical garden. It was, however, laid out in 1972. During the time of the Willet-Holthuysens, a coach house and stables were located at the present site of the garden. They didn't survive the years that since passed. Everything else at the museum seems to be defying the passage of time.

Details: Mon. to Fri., 10–5, Sat. and Sun., 11–5. Cost: fff/ee.

21 Munttoren (Mint Tower)
At Muntplein (intersection of Amstel, Rokin, Singel and Vijzelstraat)

The polygonal base of the Munttoren was originally part of the Regulierspoort, a once-famous gate in Amsterdam's medieval city wall. The wide base dates from 1490 and gets its name from the fact that for two years (1672-3) it was used as a mint; during those years the French occupied much of the rest of the Netherlands and Amsterdammers, unable to get their Rijksdollars and ductatoons from their usual source, started minting their own in the fortified base. The gate was itself destroyed by fire in 1618. The solitary clock tower with steeple atop the base was added in 1619 by master architect Hendrick de Keyser, who also designed the churches of Westerkerk, Noorderkerk and Zuiderkerk. The carillon — a set of tuned bells sounded by hammers controlled from a keyboard — was designed by François Hemony (who also designed the carillon at Oude Kerk) in 1699, and rings every 15 minutes. As a sign of the times, a pricey giftshop presently occupies the base of the tower.

Details: The base of the tower can be seen during the giftshop's normal business hours (daily, 9–5). The upper portion of the tower is closed to the public.

Bloemenmarkt (Floating Flower Market)
In Singel Canal, from Leidsestraat to Vijzelstraat

As odd as it might sound, there once was a time when a tulip was worth more than its weight in gold. The scene was Amsterdam, early 17th century, during a period called the Golden Age, when many local merchants had become, or were in the process of becoming, rich through enormously lucrative trade deals occurring on distant shores. The Amsterdam-tulip connection dates from that time, when Dutch diplomats in Turkey set eyes on the erect cup-shaped flowers and returned to the Netherlands with a pile of them. The showy flowers were a big hit, and soon the demand for them created a market. When an inquisitive botanist named Johan van Hooghelande figured out how to vary the color and shape of the blooms, the competition to create and possess the loveliest tulips was on. Soon wealthy Dutchmen throughout southern Holland no longer talked about women, but only about voluptuous, long-stemmed tulips. By 1635 Amsterdam was in the grip of a flower frenzy, and prices reflected it. For instance, records show that a farmer paid four tons of butter, four fat oxen, 1,000 lbs. of cheese, eight pigs, a dozen sheep, a bed and a suit of fine clothes for a single Viceroy tulip. Yes, some of the buyers were bonkers, but not all. With the price of tulips soaring, many people viewed the bulbous herbs as wise investments. To their dismay, the tulip futures market crashed in 1636. Within weeks many people lost their farms. But the Dutch never turned their backs on the flower, and soon after the canals were built nurserymen took to selling tulips from boats they paddled about town. Over time the flower merchants settled on a site to bring their lovely goods. Today, the so-called floating flower market still exists, but most of the flowers on sale are actually placed on a wide sidewalk, and the "boats" are permanently moored barges. The tulips, however, are truly beautiful, and they're reasonably priced; consider bringing some back to decorate your hotel room.

Details: Mon. to Sat., 9–5. It's illegal to bring tulips into the U.S., Canada and other countries.

 ### Amsterdam's Canals

*Most people conjure up images of Venice when they think of cities with canals. But in fact, Amsterdam has just as many canals – 165 of them. Four main crescent-shaped canals form concentric rings around the old city center. The **Singel**, the first of the concentric canals, was the city's original medieval moat; the other three represent urban expansion as the city edged outward during the 17th century. The **Herengracht**, or "Gentlemen's" Canal is named for the gentlemen of the East India Company who funded it. These men, eager to escape the crowds of the "congested city", built the stateliest of homes here, and the most opulent of all of Amsterdam's 17th-century architecture can be found in the **Golden Bend of the Herengracht** that stretches from Leidsegracht to the Vijzelstraat. The **Keizersgracht**, the "Emperor's Canal," honors Emperor Maximillian I, and was also considered an upscale venue when built though not on par with the Herengracht. Its finest mansions can also be found between Leidsegracht and Vijzelstraat. The **Prinsengracht**, named for William of Orange, was the least desirable of the three, serving as a barrier to the working-class Jordaan district (see annotation 31) and thus its houses are smaller than on the other two canals. Today, strolling along these canals is a must for any visitor to Amsterdam. Also, the smaller canals that crisscross these major thoroughfares are the places to discover Amsterdam's hidden treasures (ironically, some of the prettiest small canals can be found in the once downmarket Jordaan). For a great **view** of Amsterdam's canal ring, head to the **top floor of Metz and Co.** department store for a pricey pastry, but a grand panorama (Keizersgracht 455 at Leidsestraat; Mon., 11–5:30, Tues. to Sat., 9:30–5:30, to 9:30 on Thurs., Sun., 12–5:30).*

Details: You can take a **canal boat trip**, which lasts about 60 to 90 minutes. Your best departure point, where most of the companies dock, is from the inner harbor at Centraal Station (see annotation 35). Boats leave every 15–30 minutes, daily, year round. Cost: fff/ee.

 ### Antique Alley
Along Nieuwe Spiegelstraat

Amsterdam is known for its antiques and art galleries, and the greatest concentration of stores specializing in both can be found along Nieuwe Spiegelstraaat and its continuation, pretty Spiegelgracht. Find that perfect piece of 17th-century Delftware or that long lost van Gogh in the upmarket shops that line the street/canal that leads from Keizersgracht to the Rijksmuseum.

Details: Store hours are generally Mon. afternoons, Tues. to Fri., 9–6, Sat., 9–5.

Narrowest House in Amsterdam
Between 310 and 312 Singel (just north of Oude Spiegel Straat)

And just how narrow is the narrowest house in Amsterdam? About four feet. It's slightly wider than a standard exterior door. You don't need a wide-angle lens to photograph this house, which actually looks quite lovely from the street. The paint is glossy, the door latch wasn't cheap, the little windows are kept very clean, and the curtains behind them effectively block prying eyes. That's about all that can be said about the place, really, because except for the doorway, which is wedged between two much larger houses, there's little more to see. Disturbing the occupants to ask them if a total stranger can roam about their tiny house certainly wouldn't be good form. But if you've come to Amsterdam to see some sights and you happen to be in the area of this slight home, stop by and take a look. Words really don't do it justice. This much can be said for the place: Within a year you may forget what the Rijksmuseum looks like, but you aren't likely to forget the façade of this house any time soon.

Details: Please refrain from knocking on the door of the narrowest house in town. The owners will not welcome the intrusion.

Bijbels Museum (Bible Museum)
Herengracht 366; Tel: 020/624-2436

If you've just visited the narrowest house and feel like thanking God that you don't live in a house barely wider than a refrigerator, you might find a divine ear ready to receive your prayer at the Bijbels Museum. Located in two 17th-century houses, the museum is filled with display cases containing artifacts that attempt to add historical weight to biblical passages. Here, you'll find models of religiously significant sites such as King Solomon's Temple, as well as archaeological finds from the Middle East. Also on the premises are some very old Dutch bibles (more interesting for those who speak Dutch). However, the museum is situated in two of a group of four 17th-century houses designed by master architect Philips Vingboons. The houses both contain their original kitchens and gorgeous 18th-century ceiling paintings by Jacob de Wit.

Details: Mon. to Sat., 10–5, Sun., 1–5. Cost: ff/e.

Woonbootmuseum (Houseboat Museum)
In canal opposite Prinsengracht 296 (near Elandsgracht); Tel: 020/427-0750

The canals of Amsterdam contain scores of houseboats, and if you're ever wondered what they look like inside, here's your chance to find out. The museum is set in the Hendrika Maria, *a former commercial sailing ship built in 1914 and converted into a houseboat. The deckhouse, where the skipper's family resided, is just as it was when the family packed up and, presumably, shoved off. The former cargo hold was made into a fairly comfortable living area, with all the cramped conveniences (the toilet does indeed empty directly into the canal, which is typical of the houseboats throughout Amsterdam; the canals are "flushed" on a regular basis to keep the city from acquiring an unpleasant smell). Ship models, photos and a brief slide show round out the experience. Antique lovers can head to the nearby* **De Looier Kunst & Antiekcentrum**, *a multi-stall antique market. You never know what will turn up in this vast maze of vintage Delftware, antique furniture, Art Deco lamps and the like (109 Elandsgracht).*

Details: Tues. to Sun., 10–5. Cost: ff/e.

HELPFUL HINTS

GETTING AROUND

To and From Schiphol Int'l Airport: Amsterdam's international airport is located 11 miles southwest from the city center. Traveling between the airport and downtown is easy. The simplest (and most expensive) way to reach downtown is by taxi. Taxis can be found in front of the terminal (f65 each way). Another option is to hop on one of the KLM Sky Liner buses, also located just outside the terminal. The buses operate between the airport and particular hotels, but you don't have to be a guest of any of the specified hotels to take advantage of the service. There are two painted lines beside the buses — an orange one and a yellow one. The orange line serves the Dam Square area, stopping at the Pulitzer, Victoria, Sonesta, Krasnapolsky and Barbizon Palace hotels. The yellow line serves Leidseplein and southern areas, stopping at the Amsterdam Hilton, the Ibis, Parkhotel, Barbizon Centre and the Amsterdam Apollo. The buses depart every 30 minutes from 6:25 a.m. to 11:25 p.m (f20 each way). The third option is to catch a train headed to Centraal Station. These trains leave at 15-minute intervals from 5 a.m. to 1 a.m. and hourly from 1 a.m. to 5 a.m. The clean, safe trains can be boarded from a platform reached by an escalator located near the center of the terminal (f6).

In Amsterdam: Getting around Amsterdam is a snap. Because the city center is so compact, it can be easily walked — provided you've got good legs. The city is also well served by **trams**, most of which originate from several stops located in front of Centraal Station. Trams can be boarded throughout the downtown area from any of the tram stops. It's always a good idea to enter using the tram's rear door, as the ticket booth is located at the back of the tram. Regardless of how far you go, the cost of a tram ride is f3; you can also buy a strip of tickets for less per ride; strippenkaart). Trams operate from 6 a.m. weekdays (7 a.m. weekends) until midnight daily. Keeping slightly later hours (4 a.m. until 2 a.m. daily) is the city's fleet of **buses**. Unlike the trams, riders are required to enter at the front of the vehicle. Buses follow the same routes as the trams, but they're not nearly as popular. Be advised that no public transportation is available between 2 a.m. and 4 a.m. (except for taxis). **Taxis** can be found all over the city, but due to the high cost of gasoline they do not cruise the streets in search of potential customers. If you want a taxi, you must approach its driver. The city's major taxi stands are located at Centraal Station, Dam Square, Elandsgracht, Leidseplein, Muziektheater, Nieuwmarkt, Rembrandtsplein, Spui and Tropenmuseum. You can also take a **canal ride** to get an overview of Amsterdam's most famous assets. Boats leave daily, every 15-30 minutes from in front of Centraal Station (see annotation 35). You can combine a canal trip with a museum visit by hopping on and off the **museum boat**, which cruises the waterways stopping at or near 20 museums (daily ticket: f22 with up to 50% discount on museum admission). The **tourist information office** is located across from Centraal Station.

SPECIAL SUGGESTIONS

The following special suggestions will make your stay in Amsterdam even more memorable:
- View the finest of paintings by Rembrandt and Vermeer (see annotation 1).
- Learn about van Gogh's tragic life and admire one of the world's best collections of his paintings (see annotation 2).
- Take a walk on the chic side on P.C. Hooftstraat (see annotation 6).
- Tour the Heineken Brewery and taste why it is one of the city's top attractions (see annotation 7).
- Check out the Times Square of Amsterdam, home to lovely cafés and lively clubs (see annot. 8).
- Spend an hour or two in the Tropics (see annotation 10).
- Tour Amsterdam's impressive Jewish Historical Museum (see annotation 14).
- Visit the hiding place of the most famous diarist in the world (see annotation 29).
- Meander the picturesque streets of the Jordaan district (see annotation 31).
- Brighten your day with a trip to the Aalsmeer Flower Auction (see "Quick Trips").

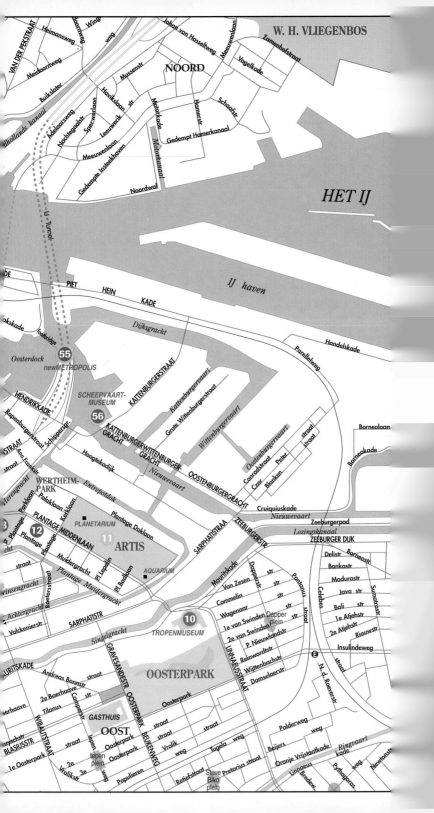

QUICK TRIPS

HAARLEM

With the exception of some tourists, little has changed on the quiet streets of quaint Haarlem since medieval times. This picture-perfect town boasts a sprinkling of Dutch almshouses (some dating to the 14th century), and is known throughout Holland for its excellent Frans Hals Museum (Groot Heiligland 62; Mon. to Sat., 11–5, Sun., 1–5; Cost: ff/e; Tel: 023/516-4200). Hals's best works are in this museum, displayed in galleries that approximate the rooms of a 17th-century mansion. Most notable are his Civic Guard portraits, seen in rooms like those the artist had in mind for them. Also not to be missed is the magnificent Christiaan Müller Organ of Grote Kerk (Oude Groenmarkt 23; Mon. to Sat., 10–4; tel: 023/532-4399), built in 1735 and one of Europe's finest organs. Mozart and Händel both made special trips to Haarlem just to play the ornately carved, 5,068-pipe instrument. Free concerts are given every Tues. and Thurs. from April to October; hours vary.

Details: 15 miles west of Amsterdam via N5 and A5. Trains run from Centraal Station every half hour to Haarlem (trip takes about 20 minutes).

EDAM

Edam is every bit as charming as Amsterdam — and far less crowded. Like the much larger city, Edam is criss-crossed with picturesque canals. Across these waterways are storybook drawbridges, and flanking the canals are quaint teahouses, lovely canal houses and gardens exploding with tulips. And, yes, this is the city after which Edam, the cheese, was named. You'll find it here sealed in yellow wax (Edam coats its export cheese in red wax). Cheese lovers visiting Edam during July and August will want to time their arrival for the town's kaasmarkt (cheese market), located in the main square and open Wednesdays from 10:30 a.m. to 12:30 p.m.

Details: 14 miles northeast of Amsterdam via N247. Edam has no train station but buses depart Centraal Station hourly throughout the day.

AALSMEER FLOWER AUCTION (BLOEMENVEILING)

The Dutch are the world's largest flower exporters and this mammoth complex is the spot where they auction off their prized wares. In this warehouse the size of 90 football fields, exporters snap up cut flowers at a rate of 14 million+ per day. And while you can't take part in the auction, you can watch the action as rows of bidders sitting in four enormous auction halls place their bids by pushing buttons. The bidders respond to bunches of flowers and plants that are wheeled by in carts. Some 600 lots are sold this way every hour. Auctioning is done from high to low (as opposed to from low to high), so the first buyer to push a button walks off with the goods. The action is fast and furious, and a whole lot of fun to watch. Plus the millions of flowers assembled in the space below the viewing gallery is a sight you will never forget. And if you're in Holland in April, catch the bulbfields at **Keukenhof**, a 70-acre park with 7 million flowers in bloom. Awesome! (late Mar.-May, daily, 8-7:30; tel: 025/246-5555 to confirm; continue on A 4 and take the Lisse exit).

Details: Mon. to Fri., 7:30 a.m.–11 a.m. Admission: fff/ee. 12 miles southwest of Amsterdam via A4 (near Schiphol Airport). Reached by Bus 172 from Centraal Station.

LEIDEN (not shown on back cover map)

Leiden bills itself as Holland's "Museum City" and with 14 museums it's got every right to. The Lakenhal, set in a 17th-century Guild Hall, offers exceptional works by Dutch Masters (daily, 10-5). The Antiquities Museum, in Leiden's old quarter, has a fine sampling of mummies and Roman fragments (Tues. to Sat., 10-5, Sun., 12-5). And at the Leiden American Pilgrim Museum you'll note that the Pilgrims made Leiden their last stop before sailing to the New World. Leiden is also famous for its university, founded in 1581, and the most picturesque, and oldest, area is around the Rapenburg canal, where you'll also find many of the university buildings that give Leiden its collegiate air.

Details: 25 miles southwest of Amsterdam via A4. Trains run from Centraal Station to Leiden on a frequent basis (trip takes about 35 minutes).

Legend

- **Historic Landmark**
- **Best Museum**
- **Superior Shopping**
- **Hidden Treasure**
- **Child's Sight**
- **Also Very Good for Children**
- **i** Tourist Information
- — Tram Lines
- — Pedestrian-only Streets

0   250 Meters

250 Feet

N
W ← → E
S

CENTRAL AMSTERDAM (enlarged)

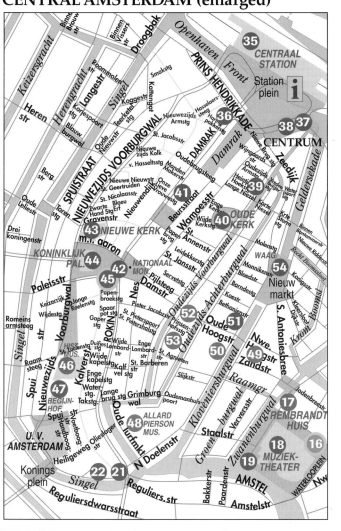

TripBuilder®

Westerkerk (West Church)
Westermarkt at Prinsengracht (near Raadhuisstraat); Tel: 020/624-7766

*The Renaissance-style Westerkerk was designed by Hendrick de Keyser (who also designed Noorderkerk, Zuiderkerk and Munttoren), but he died well before the church was consecrated in 1631. Keyser's son, Pieter, supervised Westerkerk's completion. The sober Protestant interior is brightened by a massive organ with colorful scenes of a dancing King David and a voluptuous Queen of Sheba. Well above it all, at 277 feet, is the **tallest tower in Amsterdam**, and inside it, weighing 16,500 lbs, is the largest bell in the city. Atop the steeple is the red, blue and gold crown of the Holy Roman Empire, a symbol bestowed by Maximilian; Amsterdam earned the Austrian emperor's gratitude by supporting his faction in the struggle for domination of the Netherlands. And, somewhere under the floor of the church are the bones of Rembrandt van Rijn. It is certain that the Dutch Master was laid to rest in the church, but now nobody knows exactly where. Considerable work has been done on the church over the years, and it's possible the bones went out with the trash. That would explain why numerous efforts to locate them have come up empty. A memorable plaque honoring the great artist appears beside the grave of his son, Titus, who was also laid to rest in Westerkerk.*

Details: Mon. to Sat., 11–5, Sun., 1–5. Tower: June to Sept., Wed. to Sat., 10–4. Cost: ff/e.

Anne Frankhuis (Anne Frank House)
Prinsengracht 263; Tel: 020/556-7100 (www.annefrank.nl)

This is the house where Jewish teenager — and diarist — Anne Frank and her family hid from the Nazis, living in a secret annex behind a bookcase from 1942 to 1944. Anne Frank was born in Frankfurt in 1929, but when the Nazis came to power, Otto and Edith Frank moved to Amsterdam with their daughters Margot and Anne. There they lived in relative safety until 1940, when SS troops began a five-year occupation of the Netherlands. In early 1942, Germany began ordering Amsterdam's Jewish population to report to a theater-turned-deportation center (see annotation 12), where the Jews had been told they would be transported to Germany to work in factories. Instead, the trains took them to concentration camps, where most of the Jews were killed. On July 6, 1942, a day after Margot received a call-up notice "to report to work," the Frank family went into hiding. The war couldn't last forever, and the Franks hoped to wait it out in the secret annex of the building where Otto had worked. A week later Hermann and Auguste van Pels and their son Peter joined them. In November, the dentist Fritz Pfeffer arrived. The annex inhabitants were helped by Otto's four former employees. Soon after the hiding began, Anne celebrated her 13th birthday and Otto's present to her was a diary. For the next 2 years she recorded her most intimate thoughts in the diary. Her fondest wish was to become a writer. "After the war I'd like to publish a book called 'The Secret Annex' ... my diary can serve as the basis," she wrote on May 11, 1944. Three months later the hiding place was betrayed. No one knows by whom. The annex inhabitants were taken away, and Anne's diary pages were left behind. A few hours later one of the helpers, Miep Gies, found the journal and kept it. Of all of the annex inhabitants only Otto Frank survived the camps (Anne died of typhus at Bergen-Belsen in March 1945, a few weeks before the camp was liberated). In June 1945, Otto Frank returned to Amsterdam, and Miep gave Otto his daughter's diary. For the first time he read everything Anne had written, and he determined to have it published. The diary first appeared in book form in 1947. Since then, it has been translated into 60 languages. The annex, with its tiny rooms with faded floral wallpaper and narrow passageways, has survived intact and is open for public viewing. Even the photos Anne snipped from magazines and taped to the wall of her tiny room are still there. Also on view are Anne's diary and photos of the young woman taken during happy times.

Details: Apr.–end Aug., daily, 9–9; Sept–end May, daily, 9–5. Cost: fff/ee. This is one of the city's most visited sights so be prepared for crowds in summer and go early.

Theatermuseum
Herengracht 168-174 (north of Raadhuisstraat); Tel: 020/551-3300

The Netherlands Theater Institute exists to contribute to the knowledge of the Dutch theater culture. To this end, it has created a Theatermuseum on the ground floor of its Herengracht headquarters that displays retrospective exhibitions that usually run for about two years. These are generally very well done and contain masks, puppets, theatrical backdrops and costumes that range in age from 400 years to less than a decade. The objects make for fun viewing. Also, the institute occupies five adjoining 17th-century canal houses, one of which (No. 166) was built by Pieter de Keyser, son of master church architect Hendrick de Keyser.

Details: Tues. to Fri., 11–5, Sat. and Sun., 1–5. Cost: fff/ee.

 The Jordaan District
Bounded by Brouwersgracht, Leidsegracht, Lijnbaansgracht and Prinsengracht

This is one of the oldest parts of Amsterdam, and also one of its most charming. Quite a feat considering centuries ago the Jordaan was home to very smelly tanneries and breweries that were restricted to operating outside the upscale canal belt (see annotation 23). Today the area contains a lot of picturesque, small canals lined with centuries-old gabled houses, particularly in the area north of Rozengracht. Small cafés, antique stores and art galleries abound as do hidden garden courtyards called hofjes (unfortunately none are open to view). The best way to explore the district is: from Café Chris (see annotation 32), head up to Egelantiersgracht (the district's main canal), then zig and zag your way on the smaller side streets towards Noorderkerk (see annotation 33), and then take a stroll on Brouwersgracht (or Brewer's Canal), named for the many brewers who traded here centuries ago. Located on the northern edge of the Jordaan, this tree-lined waterway is one of Amsterdam's prettiest.

Details: Store hours are generally Mon. afternoons, Tues. to Fri., 9–6, Sat., 9–5.

 Café Chris
Bloemstraat 42 (across the canal from Westerkerk); Tel: 020/624-5942

There are two kinds of bars/cafés in Amsterdam: browns and whites. The whites are the new bars – places with new furniture, bright lights, high ceilings, modern decor and generally white walls. There's one on practically every corner. The browns are quite the opposite in appearance: the furniture is old, the lights always dim, the ceilings too low for tall hats on tall people, the decor might kindly be described as rustic, and the walls are always lined with dark wooden paneling. Which are better is a matter of opinion. Which are historic is not subject to debate. Lots of bars/cafés (most bars here have "café" in their name) claim to be Amsterdam's oldest. Of course, only one brown can wear that title, and that bar is Café Chris. The bar opened in 1624 to quench the thirsts of workers constructing nearby Westerkerk. It was also where the workers picked up their pay, and then spent it. Beer's been flowing at Café Chris since then. The place isn't big. In fact, the bathroom is so small it hasn't room for a cistern; to flush the toilet you pull a chain dangling from a cistern located outside the lavatory and practically at the center of the bar. The same cistern has been used since 1624. There's a pool table, a cigarette machine, a jukebox, a few tables and a corner bar with steins suspended from the ceiling, and little else. Every Sunday afternoon the tiny place fills with people who've come for the traditional **opera singalong***. What the one-room bar with only a half-dozen stools and several wooden tables lacks in amenities it makes up with in atmosphere every Sunday. If you want to get a taste of traditional Amsterdam, catch Café Chris on the day of rest.*

Details: Daily, 2 p.m.–1 a.m. Opera singalong: Sun., 3–8. Other **area brown bars** can be found along Prinsengracht between Bloemstraat and Westerstraat.

Noorderkerk (North Church)
Noordermarkt 44 (at Prinsengracht); Tel: 020/626-6436

Noorderkerk was the last church designed by master architect Hendrick de Keyser, and it dates from 1623. It's quite different from the much larger and grandiose Westerkerk and Zuiderkerk, which he also designed. This is a Maltese Cross-style church, the first of its kind to be built in Amsterdam. The four small houses tucked into the corners of the church shouldn't be there; they were added years later by Amsterdammers who hated to see the space go to waste. The church's shape and centrally located pulpit permit every member of the congregation, seated in encircling pews, to hear well and see well. The church, which was built as a place of worship for the poor people of the Jordaan neighborhood, still has a strong congregation. On the south facade of the brick structure is a plaque commemorating a Feb. 1941 strike called to protest the Nazi's announcement to deport the city's Jews. A service is held at the church on May 4 of every year to remember the Jews who died in World War II.

Details: Sat., 11–1. Services are held Sun., 10 and 7.

West Indisch Huis (West India House)
Herenmarkt (near Wieringerstraat and Brouwersgracht)

The four-story West Indisch Huis, now home to various offices and a banquet facility, was where the Dutch West India Company had its headquarters. The company was founded in 1624 as a weaker copycat of the extremely profitable Dutch East India Company, which was founded 22 years earlier and conducted trade with Dutch colonies in Indonesia, Africa and Asia. The West India Company controlled Dutch trade between Africa and the Americas, and was lucrative during the slave trade. But the company spent most of its profits fighting colonial battles with the Spanish and Portuguese, and it lost its chief colony — that of Nieuw Amsterdam — to the British in 1664. The British renamed the settlement and ever since it's been known as New York. Today, only the courtyard looks much the way it did when the Dutch West India Company was in business (the façade of the building was rebuilt during the 19th century). There's a memorial in the courtyard honoring Peter Stuyvesant, the mean-spirited governor of Nieuw Amsterdam whose greatest claim to fame was surrendering the island to the British. Nearby, check out **De Poezenboot (The Cat Boat)**, *a canal boat for stray cats that's owned and managed by a handful of cat lovers. At any one time up to 80 felines can be found hanging out there, either lounging in baskets or strutting about looking mischievous (In the canal, opposite Singel 40, near Brouwersgracht; daily, 1–4; tel: 020/625-8794).*

Details: The courtyard is open for viewing during the day.

Centraal Station
At the north end of Damrak; Tel 020/620-2266

Amsterdam's train station is a sight to behold. Completed in 1889 and covering an area the size of six football fields, Centraal Station is neo-Gothic in style, with steep roofs, many dormers, and lots of gold and colored decoration. In a tribute to the city's past, the façade also contains numerous maritime scenes. Twin towers flank the entryway, giving the structure a formal and symmetrical appearance. The gilded "clock" in the west tower contains not an hour hand but a weather vane that indicates wind direction (again in tribute to the city's past, when so much of its livelihood depended on trade conducted by sailing ships). The station is itself "on the sea" - the entire thing rests on 8,600 wooden piles sunk into three artificial islands. Behind the station and pretty much out of sight are the docks, which are still very much in use. As it was when it opened, the train station remains a major hub *of activity, linking Amsterdam with the rest of the country, parts of Europe, and now the international airport. The station was designed by Petrus Josephus Herbertus Cuypers, the same fellow who designed the Rijksmuseum. Many of the **canal boat tours** leave from here daily, approximately every half hour, year round (see also annotation 23; Cost: fff/ee), and there is a **tourist information office** located across the street.*

Details: The station is open 24 hours. Frequent public-service announcements in the train station warning of pickpockets there should not go unheard.

 ### Sex Museum
Damrak 18 (near Centraal Station); Tel: 020/622-8376

You can stop giggling now. Amsterdam's Sex Museum is actually rather impressive. Yes, there are zillions of hardcore sex photos and booths where porn films play endlessly. But there's also a large amount of high-quality art you just won't see at other museums: sex scenes exquisitely carved on scrimshaw dating from the 19th century; 19th-century meer-schaum pipes with finely carved embraces; a naughty carved ivory triptych from Italy, circa 1850. All of the objects are well displayed, and signage is in Dutch and English. This sprawling, multi-level museum is very popular and filled with pleasant surprises.

Details: Daily, 10 a.m.-11:30 p.m. Cost: ff/e. Signage is in Dutch and English.

 ### Schreierstoren (Weeping Tower)
Corner of Geldersekade and Prins Hendrikkade

Erected in 1480, the Schreierstoren is a stout brick tower that was once part of Amsterdam's original fortifications. Most of those fortifications were demolished during the 17th century, when the city outgrew its medieval boundaries. The Schreierstoren survived, and today it houses a shop. Just how the tower acquired its name is a bit of a mystery, but the explanation that makes the most sense is also the most romantic. In medieval times, the Schreierstoren commanded the best view of the ships at port. It was where a good many women waved and weeped as their men headed out to sea. Hence, as the story goes, it came to be known as the Weeping Tower.

Details: There's a plaque on the side of the tower honoring Henry Hudson. From here, in 1609, he left to find a direct route to the East Indies and found Nieuw Amsterdam (New York) instead.

 ### Sint Nicolaaskerk (St. Nicholas's Church)
Prins Hendrikkade 73 (corner St. Olofspoort); Tel: 020/624-8749

St. Nicholas is considered the patron saint of seafarers, but only a small model of a ship set above the back door indicates that this church was built for seamen. Appropriately, this beautiful church, with its stately neo-Renaissance façade, its captivating murals, its coffered ceiling arches and its marvelous stained glass, is located on the waterfront. The church was completed in 1887 on the site of two clandestine Catholic churches that were set up when Amsterdam was officially Protestant. Sint Nicolaaskerk is well worth a look. It is also here, every Mar. 15, that a silent procession commemorating Amsterdam's "miracle" ter-minates. To learn what that's all about, visit the Amsterdams Historisch Museum (see annotation 46).

Details: Apr.-Oct., Mon. to Fri., 11-4, Sat., 2-4.

Museum Amstelkring
Oudezijds Voorburgwal 40 (near Oude Kerk); Tel: 020/624-6604

From 1578 until 1795, the Calvinistic leadership of Amsterdam prohibited all public worship except in the Protestant churches of the Reformed tradition (which had as its central tenets the belief in the absolute sovereignty of God and the doctrine of justification by faith alone). As a result, Catholics and members of other religions set up clandestine houses of worship in private homes, which was tolerated as long as there was nothing outside the houses that indicated the churches within them. As a result, dozens of hidden churches were established. Most were Catholic and furnished in Flemish baroque style. They were generally ornate and churchlike – with pews and altars and all the other trappings of a typical church. Today, only a handful of the clandestine churches have survived, and only one – the Museum Amstelkring – remains in its original form. The church, which was constructed in the attic of a merchant's house, contains a lovely altar, a wooden statue of Mary, and many liturgical objects used in church services. The museum also contains numerous 17th and 18th-century period rooms that are simply splendid.

Details: Mon. to Sat., 10–5, Sun., 1–5. Cost: ff/e. Signage is in Dutch and English.

Oude Kerk (Old Church)
Oudekerksplein 1 (beside Oudezijds Voorburgwal); Tel: 020/624-9183

More than three centuries passed before the Oude Kerk – the earliest parish church in Amsterdam – attained its present form. The church has almost as many chapels as there have been building phases. The first phase (construction that took place during the late 13th century) has been completely lost to time. Building and alterations occurred throughout the 14th and 15th centuries. The Oude Kerk was violently looted and allowed to fall into disrepair during the Calvinistic period, from 1578 to 1795. Restorations took place during the 19th century and from 1912 to 1914, but by 1955 the whole thing was in danger of collapsing and was closed. The impressive, late-Gothic-style building reopened in 1979 and has remained open ever since. Highlights include the great organ, which dates from 1724, and the tower, which was built in 1566 and is worth a climb for its amazing **view.**

Details: <u>Church</u>: Daily, 11–4. <u>Tower</u>: June–Aug., Wed. to Sat., 2–4. Cost: ff/e. A free English-language guide is available upon request at the ticket counter.

Beurs van Berlage (Old Stock Exchange)
Damrak 213-277 (between Dam Sq. and Centraal Station); Tel 020/626-8936

Amsterdam's former stock exchange was designed by master architect Hendrik Petrus Berlage and represented a major break from 19th-century architecture when it opened in 1903. The block-long building, with its relatively plain yet powerful and modern appearance, paved the way for the world-famous Amsterdam school of architecture. Details include exquisite stained glass, Persian quatrains, tile pictures and sculptures. The building no longer functions as the stock exchange, and is now an exhibition and concert center. It is beautifully maintained, and visitors are allowed to wander through the old trading, meeting and storage rooms. The original furniture is on display, as are all of the building's original blueprints. Visitors can even enter the exchange's attic and ascend a staircase to the bell tower, which offers excellent 360-degree **views** *of central Amsterdam. Architecture buffs can easily spend half a day here.*

Details: Tues. to Sun., 10–4. Cost: ff/e.

Dam Square
Corner of Damrak and Paleisstraat

*Dam is Amsterdam's most significant square, and a hub of activity both day and night. It's flanked to the north by **Nieuwe Kerk** (see annotation 43), to the west by the **Royal Palace** (see annotation 44), to the south by **shops** (see below), and to the east by the **National War Monument**, which honors Dutch victims of World War II. The center of the wide square, which takes its name from a dam that was demolished centuries ago, is barren except for a dozen benches, scores of people and an omnipresent queue of taxis. As far back as the 17th century, if you were in Dam Square, needed a lift and could afford one, you hailed a taxi — then a horse-drawn sled. Dam's taxis of our time are Mercedes-Benz sedans, a fact that will likely make someone smile 300 years from now. The square always contains people, most of whom have come to watch other people, including — usually — some street performers. The square is also home to Amsterdam's best known department store, **De Bijenkorf** (the closest you'll get to Bloomingdales or Harrods; Dam 1; tel: 020/621-8080). From the square you can head down **Rokin**, one of Amsterdam's prime shopping streets, with upmarket venues like Sotheby's.*

Details: Police say Dam Square is a favorite of pickpockets and purse snatchers.

 Nieuwe Kerk (New Church)
Northwest corner of Dam Square; Tel: 020/638-6990

Dating from the end of the 14th century, Nieuwe Kerk was erected to replace the much smaller Oude Kerk, which was no longer able to accommodate Amsterdam's rising Catholic population. Ironically, it is a Protestant feature — a pulpit that was added when Calvinists ruled the city — and not an altar that is the focal point of the interior. Whereas the altar is always front and center in a Catholic church, the pulpit (in this case a large, flamboyantly carved pulpit surrounded by box pews) commands the congregation's attention at Nieuwe Kerk. Also noteworthy are the stained-glass windows designed in 1898 depicting Queen Wilhelmina's coronation, an elaborately adorned gilded organ dating from 1645, and a majestic three-tiered brass candelabra dating from the 17th century.

Details: Mon. to Sat., 11–4, Sun., 12–2. Cost: ff/e.

 Koninklijk Paleis (Royal Palace)
West end of Dam Square; Tel: 020/624-8698

The Royal Palace was constructed during the mid-17th century as Amsterdam's City Hall. Today, the magnificent structure serves as a reminder of Amsterdam's days of glory, reflecting the confidence of the city's residents at the height of the Golden Age, when Amsterdam was one of the world's trade centers. The building's facade is Classical, its interior filled with furnishings that bespeak wealth and power. Most impressive is the illustrious Citizen's Hall on the second level, a majestic room with a 95-foot ceiling and a marble floor inlaid with enormous bronze maps of the Eastern and Western Hemispheres. As they wandered through the hall, the 17th-century Amsterdammers crossed the world — just as many of the city's merchants and seamen actually did as they scoured the Earth for riches. Above the hall entrance, the symbolic figure of Amsterdam sits enthroned. She regards the world at her feet. The palace is filled with such artwork, all of it impressive and all of it conveying the confidence that pervaded Amsterdam at the time. When the French occupied the Netherlands in the early 19th century, Louis Bonaparte (Napoleon's brother) turned this into a royal palace and it is now used by the Dutch Royal Family for official functions (the royals prefer to live just outside The Hague).

Details: Oct. to May, Tues. to Thurs., 1–4. June to Sept., daily, 12:30-5. Cost: ff/e.

Madame Tussaud's Scenerama
Dam Square 20 (corner Damrak and Paleisstraat); Tel: 020/622-9949

Tina Turner, Vincent van Gogh, Elvis Presley, Oprah Winfrey, Anthony Hopkins, Michael Jackson, Einstein, Picasso, Churchill, Schwarzenegger, etc., etc. They're all here, waxing poetic — well, being waxy anyway. The lifesize figures look real enough, but are they really worth the time and the price of admission in a city brimming with historic attractions? A lot of people think so. There's nearly always a line at possibly the only place in the world where you'll see likenesses of the Pope, William of Orange, Benny Hill and Queen's Freddie Mercury hanging out together.

Details: Sept. to June, daily, 10–5:30; July and Aug., daily, 9:30–7:30. Cost: fff/ee.

Amsterdams Historisch Museum (Historical Museum)
Kalverstraat 92 and Nieuwezijds Voorburgwal 359; Tel: 020/523-1822

Located in the beautifully restored 17th-century buildings of the former city orphanage, the Amsterdam Historical Museum presents the city's history in an imaginative and entertaining way. One of the exhibits consists of a large floor map that lights up in sections, indicating the expansion of the city from its founding to the present. In other rooms visitors are treated to paintings of Amsterdam by Dutch Masters. The paintings are arranged in chronological order, so that as you pass from one to another you can see how the city progressed from being a fishing village to the major metropolis it is today. At the Civic Guards' Gallery you can see massive guild group portraits commissioned in the 16th and 17th centuries. Also worth seeing is a room entirely devoted to Amsterdam's "miracle," which, bizarre as the story sounds, has lots of believers: In 1345 the communion was brought to a sick man. In the evening he threw up. The vomit, which contained the host, was tossed into a fire. The host reportedly floated above the fire, undamaged by the flames. A chapel was built upon the site of the miraculous upchuck. Word of the event quickly spread, and for more than 500 years Roman Catholics flocked to the chapel to pray beside the host. The chapel burned in 1908, but once again the regurgitated sacred wafer allegedly defied the destructive force of fire. The wafer was moved to Sint Nicolaaskerk and has been there ever since. Every Mar. 15, believers from all over the world walk in silence along the Heiligeweg and up to Sint Nicolaaskerk to celebrate Amsterdam's miracle.

Details: Mon. to Fri., 10–5, Sat. and Sun., 11–5. Cost: fff/ee. Signage in Dutch only. Free museum guides in English are available upon request from the ticket counter.

Begijnhof
On Spui (just east of Nieuwezijds Voorburgwal)

There once was a sisterhood of pious women called Begijntjes who lived like nuns and often worked in convents but who never took monastic vows. Beginning in the early 14th century and for centuries thereafter, some of these women tended to a cluster of homes in Amsterdam that provided shelter for the city's homeless. The poorhouses, near the intersection of Spui and Nieuwezijds Voorburgwal, were collectively called Begijnhof. Fires ravaged Amsterdam on several occasions since this Begijnhof was constructed, but each time the three-story structures escaped the flames. They also escaped the intolerance of the Calvinists that lasted from the late 16th century till the late 18th century. The Begijnhof comprises the oldest houses in Amsterdam. The homes, most of which have been remodeled — only one still has a wooden facade — are privately owned and not open for touring (the last of the Begijntjes passed away in 1971). Still, seeing the lovely buildings with their steep roofs and tiny gardens is a treat. And after seeing the home with the rustic wooden exterior, it takes little effort to imagine how Amsterdam must have looked during the 14th century – back when wood was the dominant building material. Today, all but a few of the city's homes are made of brick and concrete. That's because, following a fire that swept through the city in 1452, legislation was passed heavily restricting the use of wood in construction. Visitors won't want to overlook the church in the courtyard. Some historians believe that America's Pilgrim Fathers may have worshiped there before setting sail to the New World. The church is occasionally open to the public.

Details: The courtyard is open daily, 9–4.

 ### Allard Pierson Museum
Oude Turfmarkt 127 (opposite Rokin); Tel: 020/526-2556 (www.uva.nl)

This museum displays the archaeological collection of the University of Amsterdam. Among the collection are some outstanding artifacts, including jewelry, weapons, statuettes, vases and cuneiform tablets that offer a glimpse of daily life in Iran, Mesopotamia, Syria, Palestine and Anatolia between 5000 BC and 800 AD. Also on exhibit are statues, portraits in stone, small bronzes, household wares and jewelry from Ancient Greece. In addition, the museum places a spotlight on Ancient Egypt, showing a model of the Pyramid of King Cheops at Giza, two mummies and lots of funerary objects. The collections could be better displayed, but fortunately much of the signage is in English as well as Dutch.

Details: Tues. to Fri., 10–5, Sat. and Sun., 1–5. Cost: ff/e.

 ### Zuiderkerk (South Church)
Zuiderkerkhof 72; Tel: 020/622-2962

The Calvinist leadership of Amsterdam took over many Catholic churches beginning in 1578 and the ones they didn't destroy they used as their own houses of worship. Central to their religion was their belief that human beings were incapable of free will after the fall of Adam, and that certain persons were elected by God to salvation, while others were rejected by him and consigned to eternal damnation. To "spread the good word," in a manner of speaking, the Calvinists built Zuiderkerk, their first church in Amsterdam (not including all the ones they stole from the Catholics). It was designed by master architect Hendrick de Keyser and consecrated in 1614, 11 years after construction on it began. Zuiderkerk's most notable feature is its soaring spire with its decorative Ionic columns and its clusters of slightly oriental pinnacles. The church made an enormous impression upon English architect Christopher Wren, who designed London's St. Paul's Cathedral as well as 52 other churches in England's capital during the mid-17th century. No offense to English architecture buffs who view Wren in the same way American architecture buffs view Frank Lloyd Wright, but Zuiderkerk is the reason why so many Christopher Wren buildings look the way they do; he borrowed rather liberally from de Keyser. Ironically, Zuiderkerk isn't nearly as popular as St. Paul's Cathedral. In recent years Zuiderkerk was attracting so few worshippers that the city gutted the structure and installed a little-visited information center dedicated to Amsterdam's urban planning. If you were an Amsterdammer wondering if the city had any plans to widen a particularly congested street, this is where you'd come to find out. The information center occasionally houses temporary exhibitions, but unless you're really interested in urban planning they won't likely be of interest to you.

Details: Mon., Tues., Wed. and Fri., 12–5.

50 **Oost Indisch Huis (Dutch East India House)**
Oude Hoogstraat 24 (at Kloveniersburgerwal)

The prosperity Amsterdam enjoyed during its Golden Age was the product of trade, and most of that trade was organized by the Dutch East India Company, the world's first multi-national corporation. The corporation maintained its headquarters at Oost Indisch Huis, beside the Kloveniersburgwal canal. Designed by master architect Hendrick de Keyser, the once-stately building with a red-brick façade is now located in Amsterdam's red light district and is showing its age. Just how grand the Oost Indisch Huis might once have been is difficult to tell. The building was completed in 1605, but no sooner had it opened than expansion plans were in the works. The first expansion occurred in 1606, the next in 1634, and yet another expansion took place in 1661 — each time to create more storage space for the spices, porcelain and silk the company was importing from Indonesia, Africa and the Far East. A major reconstruction of the interior of the building during the 1890s wiped out whatever architectural surprises de Keyser might have placed there. However, the courtyard appears to have been left alone, and the richly decorated entrance is worth a look if you happen to be in the area.

Details: The building is now part of the University of Amsterdam. It's possible to enter the courtyard during the day. The facility is locked up at night. There is no cost to enter.

51 **Rosse Buurt (Red Light District)**

Amsterdam's red light district, which covers about eight square blocks midway between Dam Square and the Muziektheater, has been around for at least 400 years. During the early 17th century, the prostitutes worked in little cubicles behind exterior doors, just as the ladies of the day and night do now. During the 1600s, the doors were made of wood and beside them the women within hung small boards painted with their likenesses. Today, the doors are made of glass and the women are visible and usually seated on bar stools — one gal per cubicle — in bikinis or lingerie. A red neon light is mounted on the window frame of all these tiny cubicles, which typically contain room for a single bed, a bar stool and a chair in which to pile your clothes. Also in the neighborhood, which is surprisingly safe due to the high police presence, are cafés that sell marijuana and hashish as menu items, video stores that sell nothing but the raunchiest pornography available, and live sex shows that typically feature women with blow guns, women who can smoke cigarettes from more than one orifice, and women with fruit. **Bananenbar** *(Oudezijds Achterburgwal 37) takes its name from the tricks its female employees perform with a particular tropical yellow fruit.* **Casa Rosso** *(Oudezijds Achterburgwal 106-108) is the most popular of the live erotic theaters, and boasts that "millions of people, couples and touristic groups, have already visited our theater, where class and creativity find its place." Uh, huh. Holding tight to the sex theme is the* **Erotic Museum** *(Oudezijds Achterburgwal 54; daily, 11 a.m.–1 a.m.; Tel: 020/524-7303), which contains five floors of mostly unimpressive and unimaginative displays; it could learn a lot from the Sex Museum on Damrak, near Centraal Station (see annotation 36). Despite its name, the red light district isn't nearly as dangerous or lecherous as you might think. Instead, it's a major tourist haunt, where spectators greatly outnumber participants.*

Details: Taking photos of the prostitutes is a major no-no. Each of the prostitutes has a "boss" who is likely to separate you and your camera forever if you try for a photo-op.

Hash Marihuana Hemp Museum
Oudezijds Achterburgwal 148 (near Damstraat); Tel: 020/263-5961

As trite as it sounds, this museum can tell you everything you could possibly want to know about hashish, marijuana and hemp. The museum features scores of well-signed, high-quality photographs of marijuana — in production and in use. There are displays devoted to the supposed medicinal values of marijuana, as well as a large section devoted to the many uses of hemp (in the manufacture of clothing, rope and so on). There are displays showing items confiscated by customs agents, such as shoes with hallowed-out heels packed with dope, sandals with an added layer of not leather but hashish, and the old no-toothpaste-in-this-full-tube trick. Of course, there are lots of museum shirts, stickers and pipes for sale, as well as a large stock of how-to-grow books. Also for sale at the ticket counter are marijuana seeds. And right there beside the ticket counter is a mirror with jail bars painted on it — a not-so-subtle reminder of how you could look if you try to smuggle marijuana or hashish into another country.

Details: Daily, 11–10. Cost: fff/ee. Note: Despite Amsterdam's lax laws pertaining to the use of soft drugs, the penalties for attempting to smuggle illegal drugs into most countries are stiff.

 Tattoo Museum
Oudezijds Achterburgwal 130; Tel: 020/625-1565 (www.tattoomuseum.com)

Amsterdam's Tattoo Museum displays many of the items you'd expect to find — plenty of books and magazines filled with tattoo designs, exhibits telling the history of tattooing and how the practice spread, a large collection of tattooing devices — but it also has a fair share of surprises. Perhaps the most impressive of them are the photos taken of tattooed people from all corners of the globe. There are captivating close-ups of heavily tattooed people in India, Nepal, Burma, Thailand, Africa, Laos, Cambodia, Japan, Taiwan, the USA, the Netherlands and a great many other places. There are close-ups of tattoos that appear on mummies, and close-ups of the tattooed inmates serving time in a Russian prison. In every instance the designs of the tattoos are easily discernable, but the photographer has also, wisely, captured the faces of the subjects and shown the subjects in their natural environment; in the photo of an Indonesian man, for example, we can see in the background much of the rustic village where he resides. The photos add a lot to this interesting and colorful museum.

Details: Daily, 12–6. Cost: ff/e. Free English-language museum guide available at the ticket counter upon request.

 De Waag (Weigh House)
In Nieuwmarkt (north end of St. Antoniesbreestraat); Tel: 020/557-9898

The Waag was built during the 14th century as part of the city's fortifications. Later, it became the location of various guilds, among them the Surgeons' Guild. Among Rembrandt's most famous paintings is one depicting a doctor dissecting a corpse with a medical student looking on. The painting, The Anatomy Lesson, *was painted in 1632 in the Theatrum Anatomicum on the second floor (unfortunately, the Theatrum Anatomicum is not open to the public). Just above the door you can still make out the guild's inscription. (There was a bricklayers' guild on the other side of the building, and if you inspect the entrance there you can see that they decorated it with a wreath of trowels.) During much of the early 17th century the stout red-brick building also served as a Weigh House. It was here that all wholesale goods brought into the city were supposed to be weighed for municipal taxes. Today the building is the site of a popular restaurant and bar that offers* free Internet access to patrons and non-patrons alike. Needless to say, the interior of the building has changed many times over the years, most recently during the early 1990s (when the restaurant was going in). The local architect in charge of that renovation attempted to capture some of the medieval feeling of the place. Most of the light in the large restaurant is provided by candles set in faux-antique holders. The tables are thick, simple in design and made of solid wood. Enormous red-velvet drapes hang beside the windows. The Waag is a great place to enjoy a coffee or a meal and absorb some splendid atmosphere.

Details: Sun. to Thurs., 10 a.m.–1 a.m., Fri. and Sat., 10 a.m.–2 a.m. Cost: Free.

newMetropolis Science and Technology Center
Oosterdok 2 (beside Valkenburgerstraat); Tel: 020/531-3233 (www.newmet.nl)

The newMetropolis is both a museum devoted to the sciences and technologies of our time and an education center, with lots of fun hands-on exhibits. In one computer-intensive area, for example, visitors are introduced to global-positioning technology, which allows users to find the exact location of any place on Earth. In a chemistry-intensive area, visitors are able to conduct experiments, such as determining how much caffeine is in a cup of coffee. Other exhibits allow visitors to study the nature of light. A less cerebral area allows children to build simple houses. This is one of those very smart museums/centers that can be appreciated by people of all ages. All that's required is a little interest in the world around us. The newMetropolis is a must-see for inquisitive minds. Architecture buffs take note: the museum, opened in 1997, was designed by Renzo Piano, famed architect of Paris's Pompidou Centre. As an added bonus, the rooftop cafe/terrace has a great **view** of the city.

Details: Sun. to Thurs., 10–6, Fri. and Sat., 10–9. Cost: fff/eee.

Nederlands Scheepvaartmuseum (Netherlands Maritime Mus.)
Kattenburgerplein 1 (near the newMetropolis); Tel: 020/523-2222

The Netherlands Maritime Museum is housed in the former National Naval Depot, which dates from the 17th century. This was where the Dutch Navy stored vast quantities of ropes, sails, compasses, weapons and other equipment. Next door are the docks where the Navy's men-of-war were built. The museum consists of 25 rooms containing more than 250,000 objects, most from the days of the Dutch East India Company and the Dutch West India Company, but there are contemporary exhibits as well. It is a fantastic museum with many awesome displays, including 70 historic boats – actual, full-size boats, not models, like the full size replica of the 17th-century East India Company ship, The Amsterdam. (To give you an idea of just how big the former naval depot is, the facility had the ability to fully provision a battle fleet of 40 ships in very little time.) The museum has ship models as well, some so magnificent they often evoke double-takes from passers-by. Also on view are many paintings that convey the colorful Netherland's maritime history in dramatic fashion. This museum is one of the largest of its kind in the world, and one of the best … a great place to spend several hours, but even several hours isn't enough time to see all this special spot has to offer.

Details: Tues. to Sun., 10–5 (also open Mon., from June 15 to Sept. 15). Cost: fff/ee.

TripBuilder®